YOUR PROMISES STAND FOREVER

JEAN CLAUDE MUSORE

ISBN-13:978-0-61545-993-6

ISBN-10:0-61545-993-5

Printed in the United States of America.

The Holy Bible, New International Version (NIV)
copyright©2011.Used by permission of Zondervan.

The New King James Version of the Bible (NKJV)
Copyright©2011.User by permission

"I hope you are going to be blessed and touched by the word of God in this book"

YOUR PROMISES
STAND FOREVER

CONTENTS

DEDICATION

Thanks be to God for saving my life after I survived massacre, torture, and other terrible circumstances during my life. God, you are my daddy in all, wherever I will go I will publish your blessing to the world.

ACKNOWLEDGMENTS

I thank my father and my mother, who gave me life. Thank you to Daddy, who is no longer alive, for teaching me the word of God since my childhood. I hope someday to meet you in Heaven, Daddy. May God reward you, wherever you are.

I thank my mom, who prayed for me day and night without ceasing, for God's blessings to continue to be manifested upon me. Mom, may God bless you.

I thank Pastor Rwegura Samson and Jose Umuhoza, who live in Rwanda. You showed me love and your courage to pray without cessation. I love you very much and God will reward you forever in your family and in your life. Your friendships made me a stronger man and helped me commit my life to God. I remember, when I first arrived in America, you prophesied some of my life experiences by phone.

To all my friends and beloved orphans, thank you also for your prayers and your common spirituality. Your advice helped me adapt to the new society I inhabit.

Special thanks to: Jessica, Carl and Joe, who have been supportive and encouraging from the beginning, helping me step by step with my work.

I would not have been able to accomplish nearly as much as I have if I lacked your assistance and friendship.

Each of the following persons has contributed to the success of my new life in California.

I have known Carl since 2010, when we were introduced by Refugee Transitions, an organization based in San Francisco that helps refugees new to America. Carl and I met regularly to discuss my projects and my new country. Carl, God will reward you in your life. I can never repay you for your dedication to this book, the drafts of which you must have read ten times before publishing!

Jessica has been a profound help to me since we first met when she was researching her own book. She has been very generous in sharing her knowledge and has worked tirelessly to help women facing persecution and challenges across the world.

I met Joe in 2007, when I first came to the Bay Area. Joe provided me critical support in 2009, before I found regular work. His kindness and generosity are extremely appreciated!

To my wife, Maombi Musore, I thank you for accepting me as your husband, and for all of your unique support to me, which no one else can provide.

To my mother-in-law, your constant admonitions that God will help in all ways and things have been of great comfort and truth. He knows you well and he listens your prayers.

Thank you to my sister Chantal N and Ingineri for all your support; guys, I love you so much.

Thank you to: Beatrice Gisaro, brother-in-law Ahadi Fiston and their family, who sponsored my civil wedding in Canada and also Amani Sebaziga, Mwiza Esther, Mukiza, Aimee Umutoni and Abdallah Munira, for sponsoring my first visit to my fiancé in Canada in May, 2009.

Author's Note

*"Trust in the LORD and do good; dwell in the land and enjoy safe pasture.
Take delight in the LORD, and he will give you the desires of your heart. Commit your way to the LORD;
trust in him and He will do this"*

-PSALM 37:3-5, NIV

INTRODUCTION

Man is a living being created with great value. God gives you a plan from birth up until the day of your death. This is what we mean when we say "God is the alpha and omega."

I have taken the initiative to write this book because God has loved me so much for my entire life, and He has given many wonderful blessings to me and to you.

Our God loves us so much and so completely. I want to show the blessings of God, the power of prayer and the plan that God has for everyone, and the importance of giving thanks to God for these things.

I believe that God has given me life so that I can share these blessings with the entire world.

I have always known that God would never leave me. It is imperative that you recognize that God loves you and that he has a plan for you.

I have written drafts of this book many times in many different situations since 2009. God loves to hear our praise and thanks. I promise that any reader who takes the time to read these words will find that God will answer. He has always done this for each of us and He always will.

I always hear people say, "Time is money." We constantly occupy ourselves with work so that we can have money to pay the rent. In my house, we work hard to pay the bills. We take what's left and send it back to our brothers, sisters and friends in Africa.

I work in a gas station as a cashier. Sometimes, either in the morning or afternoon when I break for lunch, I think about how my God loves me, and how He loves everyone.

I write my thoughts in a notebook when I have a free moment and there are no customers waiting at the pump. When I gather up all the scraps of paper I have written on and look at them together, I can begin to see the bigger testimony, and recognize that God had a plan for the day before yesterday, for yesterday, for today, tomorrow and eternity. As time passed, I found I had accumulated enough testimony to compose a small book.

When I arrived at my house after work, I opened my laptop and began to write again. I told God: "Thank you for today. I know everything comes from you. You do not fault any one of us."

Nothing in this world is perfect. I remember my father who passed away, Aaron Muvunyi, my friends and strangers who maybe were more perfect to God than I and are no longer here on this earth.

I understand that the reason I am still living in California is so that I can tell of the blessings that my God has given to me and give him thanks every day no matter where I am or what other people say or think about me.

See now, because of the grace of God, I have succeeded in writing my first book to let people near and far know how God is Good, even though many people don't yet understand how much God loves them.

I want to suggest that God has never failed to do right for each of us who live in this world. Sadly, many people do not recognize how many times God has done the right thing for us.

First, we live by the grace of God. Second, we ask for forgiveness, and are forgiven without judgment. When you read this book you will understand that God has done great things for me and can do great things for you if you take the time to thank Him for all that He has done for you.

My prayer:

I thank you God, my celestial father, for loving me, for giving me the intelligence to write of your blessings, and for the world that will know that you are God,

And everyone who does not know you by your acts will know you by the things you have done for me and my family.

I ask that you help everyone reading this book to know your blessings, give us the grace to love and help others as you have told us in the Bible.
Amen

THE IMPORTANCE OF GIVING THANKS TO GOD

"*Each of the four living creatures had six wings and was covered with eyes all around, even under its wings. Day and night they never stop saying:*

"*Holy, holy, holy, is the Lord God Almighty?*

Who was, and is, and is to come."

Whenever the living creatures give glory, honor and thanks to him who sits on the throne and who lives forever and ever."

"You are worthy, our Lord and God,
to receive glory and honor and power,
for you created all things,
and by your will they were created
and have their being."

-*REVELATION 4:8-9, 11, NIV*

If you say "thank you" to God, you will see that you receive what you need.

Secondly, when you give me something, in this case I am obligated to thank you for having received it. Sometimes, we thank our brothers, our sisters, our parents, and also our friends when they do something for us, but we forget to give thanks to God when it is God who allows all.

The Bible says:

"I will not die but live,
and will proclaim what the LORD has done."

-PSALM 118:17, NIV

For my part, I ask myself why we thank people before we thank God. We forget to give thanks to God, but ultimately, all things come from God. Although some would doubt this, it is even possible for God to provide for us directly, as told in:

- 1KING 18:37-39:

"Answer me, LORD; answer me, so these people will know that you, LORD, are God, and that you are turning their hearts back again."

Then the fire of the LORD fell and burned up the sacrifice, the wood, the stones and the soil, and also licked up the water in the trench.

When all the people saw this, they fell prostrate and cried, "The LORD—he is God! The LORD—he is God!"

Even in my own experience, having given money to a homeless man, I was saddened and confused by his profuse thanks to me. I, after all, was only a conduit for God's love. He was owed the gratitude.

I felt that was an injustice to God, who has given us so much, including life.

Many people don't know the secret of giving thanks to God.

Personally, I find I am very blessed when I take the time to thank God. It is for this reason that I say it constantly, no matter where I am, because I discovered the importance of thanking God.

I thank God that I live and breathe and can move and take actions in this world. After the death of my father, I asked myself many questions. The first answer I received was that gratitude is the answer to everything.

I am constantly astonished by how many of the people around me say they don't have the time to thank God.

Sometimes I'll ask friends or colleagues, "When was the last time you thanked God for the blessings that you have received in your life?"

They say, "I just don't have the time. I'm busy with so many things. When I get home from work at night, I'm just too tired."

"Jean-Claude, you remind us how God helped us narrowly escape being killed in 1996 and 2004, and how we should still give thanks today, but really, that's an old story that happened so long ago."

Out of the hundred friends and neighbors with whom I grew up, fewer than ten take the time to thank God daily for the blessings they have received since childhood.

To begin my daily prayer, I start by giving thanks to God for His blessings upon me, my family, and also for those who don't yet recognize the blessings of God in their lives.

Remember that God wants us to remember all of His many blessings. He is made happy by our prayers of gratitude.

When I take the time to thank God in my room, I feel tears well up in my eyes when I think of all God has done for us. I want to stand before God and tell Him of all His good works.

Some of us can remember the story of Job in the Bible, who continued to thank God despite losing his family and everything he owned.

Some say, "God, if you get me a job, if you heal me, if you protect me, then I'll give thanks to you." And then we forget those words as soon as we receive God's blessings. And when you ask people if they took the time to thank God for all the good things He has done for them, they respond, "What's the use? All that is in the past."

But God will never forget that one day you promised to thank Him.

Why not thank God, my friends? Give thanks that God blesses you; that you are alive. You eat, you sleep in peace, but you take these things for granted.

Coming close to God through prayer is wonderful. My Heart belongs to you, God.

Give thanks to Him and His blessings will increase every day and every hour.

There is no reason why I sing His praises and write this book other than to thank Him for forgiving me and giving me so much. When God forgave my sins, I said I want to sing and proclaim it wherever I am.

Even when I am troubled, I say thank you to God. Even when I am sick, I thank Him. Even when those around me hate me, He loves me and I thank Him.

Many people remember God when they have troubles, but few remember Him in times of good fortune.

Remember Job and his wealth. He remained grateful even when God stripped him of everything he had in this world.

Job said:

"Naked I came from my mother's womb,
and naked I will depart.
The LORD gave and the LORD has taken

away;
may the name of the LORD be praised."

- JOB 1:21 NIV

When you take just one minute in your room, or wherever you are, to address God, you begin to explain all of the good things that He has already done for you, for your family, for your friends, and also for the widows and orphans the world over.

Directly, my God also has plans to do more good things for you still.

In the New Testament, Jesus himself, before praying to his Father, lifted his eyes to the sky while saying, "I thank you father for this day," and only then did he pray for what he wanted.

"Taking the five loaves and the two fish and looking up to heaven, he gave thanks and broke the loaves. Then he gave them to his disciples to distribute to the people. He also divided the two fish among them all".

- MARK 6:41

I remember a woman who prayed at the same church with us in Africa. I remember how the woman in my church stood in front of the assembled worshipers one Sunday because she had asked the pastor for the chance to thank God for everything He had done for her. She was in front of the entire congregation, and she began to thank God by saying: "I am standing before you today to thank my God for everything, both the good and the bad."

The congregation looked on while murmuring and others wondered if she might be crazy.

In tears, the woman continued to speak:

"God, thank you because my child is sick, thank you because you have spared me, thank you because I am poor, thank you, thank you because I am here and I am in front of you."

When she arrived at her house, she discovered that her son was cured! Two days later, someone gave her a sealed envelope. In opening it, she discovered enough money to take care of all her needs. God had blessed her because she took the time to thank him in public.

No matter our position in life, our mistakes or achievements, all praise and thanks must be to God.

"Praise the LORD, my soul;
all my inmost being, praise his holy name.
Praise the LORD, my soul,
and forget not all his benefits—
who forgives all your sins
and heals all your diseases,
who redeems your life from the pit
and crowns you with love and compassion,
who satisfies your desires with good things
so that your youth is renewed like the
eagle's".
- PSALM 103:1-5 NIV

When I came to the United States, I thought about what gift I could give to God for all His blessings. Throughout my life, He never left me alone, in good times and bad. I was unable to think of a worthy sign of my gratitude, but I committed to Him these words:

My Lord,

Receive this thanks my king,

Receive this song my king,

I love you,

I will serve you,

I will make known the works you've done my Lord,

I will proclaim you throughout the whole world and tell of all

Your deeds for me that I cannot forget.

With what can I pay you back?

With whom can I compare you?

You give me breath for free; you give me salvation for free

You took me from ashes and made me a prince.

GOD'S PLAN FOR EACH OF US

"I make known the end from the beginning,
from ancient times, what is still to come.
I say, 'My purpose will stand,
and I will do all that I please".

- ISAIAH 46:10, NIV

God's plans operate variously and in an incredible and inscrutable manner. He does not judge us by our acts, our beauty, our size, our race or gender. He sees only kindness, as He has created man in His image.

God's plans delivered the Israelites by using a man like Moses who did not speak eloquently.

God knew this about Moses, but He did not judge his character from his ability to speak well. God appeared to him in a burning bush and said:

The LORD said, "I have indeed seen the misery of my people in Egypt. I have heard them crying out because of their slave drivers, and I am concerned about their suffering. So I have come down to rescue them from the hand of the Egyptians and to bring them up out of that land into a good and spacious land, a land flowing with milk and honey—the home of the Canaanites, Hittites, Amorites, Perizzites, Hivites and Jebusites. And now the cry of the Israelites has reached me, and I have seen the way the Egyptians are oppressing them. So now, go. I am sending you to Pharaoh to bring my people the Israelites out of Egypt."

But Moses said to God, "Who am I that I should go to Pharaoh and bring the Israelites out of Egypt?"

And God said, "I will be with you. And this will be the sign to you that it is I who have sent you: When you have brought the people out of Egypt, you will worship God on this mountain."

- EXODUS 4:7-12, NIV

As was true for Moses, the same was for my family and me. God has had a plan for me since my birth. We survived many tribulations, including massacres that left many in my tribe dead, wounded and permanently disabled. Despite being surrounded by this carnage, my mother, sister and I were protected from harm by God.

After surviving the massacres, we were but a few of seemingly millions of survivors interviewed for resettlement in United States. God knew of the manner in which I and my family would come to accept that He has a plan for each of us.

"For I know the plans I have for you,"
declares the LORD, "plans to prosper you and
not to harm you, plans to give you hope and a
future".

- JEREMIAH 29:11, NIV

From 1996 through 1998, I lived in a region called Kalemie, an area of the Congo, with my family and millions of other people like me, before the war came to where we were and many people escaped in different directions. Many of us were killed in the war, but because God has a plan for everyone, I was saved along with my mom and my sister. Do you think that I who was saved when certain friends and servants of God were not, that I am perfect compared to them? Only because God has a beautiful plan for me was I saved when they were not.

"For my thoughts are not your thoughts,
neither are your ways my ways, declares the
LORD.

As the heavens are higher than the earth,
so are my ways higher than your ways
and my thoughts than your thoughts."

- ISAIAH 55:8-9, NIV

Remember the story of Esther, an orphaned child like me and you. But God knew that one day she would be the wife of a king.

"For if you remain silent at this time, relief
and deliverance for the Jews will arise from
another place, but you and your father's
family will perish. And who knows but that
you have come to your royal position for such
a time as this?"

- ESTHER 4:14, NIV

My God never regrets or forgets his plan.

"No one will be able to stand against you all
the days of your life. As I was with Moses, so
I will be with you; I will never leave you nor
forsake you".

- JOSHUA 1:9, NIV

Reading this verse from Joshua compelled me to write of God's enduring love for us.

By leading me to write this book, God traced a plan beginning long ago, watching the journey I would take before arriving here in California. I never imagined that one day I would be here, nor could I imagine how badly so many others would seek to emigrate as I did, only to be denied that opportunity. And why? I say that God has a plan for you.

Why must you not ask how many friends are not here with us today? And why me? For what reason am I here? I believe I am here to reveal to you that God has a good plan for you, too. I am still living, doing what my father cannot now do. God also has a plan for me and my family everywhere. I will speak it without shame because it is a good plan.

Do you think that in the universe we inhabit that anyone would believe that a person could travel the Pacific Ocean inside a whale? But God traced a plan for Jonas to spend three days and nights inside a whale, and he found that he had crossed the ocean.

"Go to the great city of Nineveh and preach against it, because its wickedness has come up before me."

But Jonah ran away from the LORD and headed for Tarshish. He went down to Joppa, where he found a ship bound for that port. After paying the fare, he went aboard and sailed for Tarshish to flee from the LORD.

Then the LORD sent a great wind on the sea, and such a violent storm arose that the ship threatened to break up. All the sailors were afraid and each cried out to his own god. And they threw the cargo into the sea to lighten the ship.

But Jonah had gone below deck, where he lay down and fell into a deep sleep. The captain went to him and said, "How can you sleep? Get up and call on your god! Maybe he will take notice of us so that we will not perish."

Then the sailors said to each other, "Come, let us cast lots to find out who is responsible for this calamity." They cast lots and the lot fell on Jonah. So they asked him, "Tell us, who is responsible for making all this trouble for us? What kind of work do you do? Where do you come from? What is your country? From what people are you?"

"He answered, "I am a Hebrew and I worship the LORD, the God of heaven, who made the sea and the dry land."

"This terrified them and they asked, "What have you done?" (They knew he was running away from the LORD, because he had already told them so.)

"The sea was getting rougher and rougher. So they asked him, "What should we do to you to make the sea calm down for us?"

"Pick me up and throw me into the sea," he replied, "and it will become calm. I know that it is my fault that this great storm has come upon you."

"Instead, the men did their best to row back to land. But they could not, for the sea grew even wilder than before."

"Then they cried out to the LORD, "Please, LORD, do not let us die for taking this man's life. Do not hold us accountable for killing an innocent man, for you, LORD, have done as you pleased." Then they took Jonah and threw him overboard, and the raging sea grew calm." At this the men greatly feared the LORD, and they offered a sacrifice to the LORD and made vows to him."

"And the LORD commanded the fish, and it vomited Jonah onto dry land."

- JONAH 1:2-16, NIV and –JONAH 2:10, NIV

I still remember a time when I was at home with my family, watching the TV news on channel 4. It was Tuesday, January 7, 2009 at 8 p.m., and I was with my two sisters, my mother and my brother-in-law.

My youngest sister often falls asleep in the evening while watching channel 55 from Montana and channel 62, wanting to know what the weather will be like tomorrow.

We were watching channel 4, but my sister wanted to change to 62 to see the weather report. The broadcasters were showing the weather in California, but I began reflecting on today's modern technology, and how none of us can know about God's plan. The weatherman predicted that it would rain throughout the following day.

When I went to sleep, I told myself it would probably rain tomorrow, because that's what the weatherman said on television. Before going to sleep, I gathered an umbrella and a jacket to take to work the next morning. At 5 a.m., I boarded the bus. I arrived at work a half hour later without encountering any rain at all.

At work, I thought about the previous evening spent with my family. I told my colleague, "We worry about the weather, without worrying much about God's plan for us." At 9 a.m., there was a bright sun in the sky, and still no rain. I thanked God for continuing to watch over me: "Your work is great, and continues to inspire me to write."

"Our God is in heaven;
he does whatever pleases him."

- **PSALM 115:5, NIV**

It was sunny throughout that day, right up until sunset, without even a drop of rain. When I returned home, I asked my little sister, "Do you remember how they predicted it was going to rain all day?" Even when the forecasters are certain it will rain, God may have a different plan. And so it is with our lives. Sometimes, when you are going through a difficult time, remind yourself that God has a plan for every one of us.

My sister said to me, "Jean-Claude, that's true. My school is in the hills, where it often rains, but today the rain never came. I too am convinced that God has a plan for our family and all of us."

Continuing to today, I am proud of God and I never have fear in my life. God knows everything about me and everyone I know. He knows what we have been through and overcome. He does not ever forget you.

There are those who believe they are living entirely by their own volition. But think of your friend who is no longer alive today. There are others who are more attractive than you, richer, more educated, and those who have committed many more sins. Whatever your race or language, or whether you are rich or poor, know that God has a plan for you.

"But when God, who set me apart from my mother's womb and called me by his grace, was pleased"

- GALATIANS 1:15, NIV

TRUSTING IN HIS WIDSOM

"So is my word that goes out from my mouth:
It will not return to me empty,
but will accomplish what I desire
and achieve the purpose for which I sent it".

- ISAIAH 55:11, NIV

Eternal God, the creator of humanity and of all things, is not afraid of anything He does. He never forgets His promise; He follows through on what He says. I never forget that which He has done and what He has planned and through His benevolence we receive blessings anywhere because His wishes are those of happiness, and without God we have nothing.

Remember what He promised to our ancestors, like Abraham, father of Isaac, the Hebrews and the Arabs, father of His followers.

He knew that Abraham would have a son who would be his heir, but like us, did not believe the true followers.

Abraham was discouraged because he had become old and his wife Sara had passed the childbearing age. He was discouraged and forgot the eternal promise, but because my God never forgets what He has said, He fulfilled at a specific time what He had promised. He carried out this promise for Abraham to show him that He is my God, above all.

*Just as I, **even** with my wisdom, tell this story of Abraham, I do not believe it, but I ask God after accepting Jesus as my savior, that I also want the same promise as Abraham, but I don't understand what this promise is.*

Only through reading the Bible devotedly for more than a year did God's promises to us in it become clear to me.

"I am the LORD, and there is no other;
apart from me there is no God.
I will strengthen you,
though you have not acknowledged me,
so that from the rising of the sun
to the place of its setting
people may know there is none besides me.
I am the LORD, and there is no other.
I form the light and create darkness,
I bring prosperity and create disaster;
I, the LORD, do all these things".

- ISAIAH 45:5-7, NIV

It is not a secret. Many people don't know that this promise, addressed to them personally, is found in the Bible.

Before we had been in the United States for even a month, I became even closer to God by prayer every day, asking Him, "God, I believe you have decided that my family and I must move to the United States. Please prove to me that this is your will and that my emigration serves your purpose.

"For the revelation awaits an appointed time;
it speaks of the end
and will not prove false.
Though it linger, wait for it;
it will certainly come
and will not delay."

- HABAKKUK 2:3, NIV

When I come to a time of difficulty, I tell others what God has promised me.

"So do not fear, for I am with you;
do not be dismayed, for I am your God.
I will strengthen you and help you;
I will uphold you with my righteous right
hand."

- ISAIAH 41:10, NIV

God has many promises in each, when He speaks in the Bible; it is you and me to whom

He makes His promises. He has given my family hope.

The same is true if you are an orphan or a widow. God promises He is with you because He is the father of the orphans and the husband of widows.

"No one will be able to stand against you all the days of your life. As I was with Moses, so I will be with you; I will never leave you nor forsake you."

- JOSHUA 1:5, NIV

See, today my family is in California because of the grace of God's promise. God has never lied about what He promised you; rest only on this word which He said to you. One day someone asked of me: "Jean Claude, Do you speak or does God speak?" I responded to Him, "Yes, my God speaks as I have read in the bible."

"When you pass through the waters,
I will be with you;
and when you pass through the rivers,

they will not sweep over you.
When you walk through the fire,
you will not be burned;
the flames will not set you ablaze"

- ISAIAH43:2, NIV

Whatever we face today or will face in the future, please don't think God leaves us because we are presently experiencing difficulty.

Remember that which I showed you in your dream, and when you were praying in remote solitude, and when you were praying in your room; don't be afraid, because I never lied. This is my promise.

"Yes, and from ancient days I am he.
No one can deliver out of my hand.
When I act, who can reverse it?"

"This is what the LORD says—
he who made a way through the sea,
a path through the mighty waters,"

"Who drew out the chariots and horses,
the army and reinforcements together,
and they lay there, never to rise again,
extinguished, snuffed out like a wick:"

"See, I am doing a new thing!
Now it springs up; do you not perceive it?
I am making a way in the wilderness
and streams in the wasteland"

"The wild animals honor me,
the jackals and the owls,
because I provide water in the wilderness
and streams in the wasteland,
to give drink to my people, my chosen,"

"The people I formed for myself
that they may proclaim my praise"

- ISAIAH 43:13, 16,17,19,20 and 21, NIV

So many of us do not recognize God's promises to us. We doubt his presence and truth. On the other hand, when a fellow person promises us something, we have great confidence it will be delivered. While many human promises are broken and not delivered upon, God's promise is eternal and without doubt. This is the true meaning of this book and its title. God's promises stand forever, and He has never failed to provide. We may not understand His promises to each of us, but they are no less real or powerful because of our ignorance.

The promise that the God gave you, will be fulfilled very soon, He never changed what he promised, and even if it takes so long .he will still fulfill it.

He told Abraham that, he will give him a child, as time coming; he fulfilled and gave him a child called Isaac. And you shall wait for his promise

"Now the LORD was gracious to Sarah as he had said, and the LORD did for Sarah what he had promised. Sarah became pregnant and bore a son to Abraham in his old age, at the very time God had promised him. Abraham gave the name Isaac to the son Sarah bore him. When his son Isaac was eight days old, Abraham circumcised him, as God commanded him. Abraham was a

hundred years old when his son Isaac was born to him.

Sarah said, "God has brought me laughter, and everyone who hears about this will laugh with me." And she added, "Who would have said to Abraham that Sarah would nurse children? Yet I have borne him a son in his old age."

-GENESE 21:1-7, NIV

I can testify, He promised many things since I arrived in California. He promised me in 2007 that I would write three books, and I am glad to say today that all three books have been drafted, and that this, my first book, "**Your Promises Stand Forever**" is in your hands and I hope my second book will be published soon.

"I have spoken it, I will also bring it to pass; I have purposed it, I will also do it."

- ISAIAH46:11, KJV

THE POWER OF PRAYER

"Then you will call on me and come and pray to me, and I will listen to you." You will seek me and find me when you seek me with all your heart."

- JEREMIAH 29:12-13, NIV

I believe that prayer is the shortest and easiest path to God. Prayer does not require a lot of time. The Bible tells us that a day spent in prayer before God is worth more than a thousand years spent away from God.

In the Old Testament it seemed very difficult to speak to the Lord. Not just anyone could talk to God. Anyone who had committed a sin was obliged first to give a sacrifice and ask for forgiveness to purify them before approaching the Lord in prayer.

Don't you think that if God gave us the opportunity to be reborn into his kingdom it should be easy for us to approach his glory? We are the heirs to the kingdom of Christ. We can connect directly to God without any mediator. But we must take time to pray to God, honestly and without limits. God listens to our prayers without any impediment.

"Call to me and I will answer you and tell you great and unsearchable things you do not know"

- JEREMIAH 33:3, NIV

In 2005, I spent three days praying to God, asking him to opening a door for me to come to the USA. God answered me after one year and eight months and I am in California today.

The first night we arrived in the United States, my mom, my sister and I prayed to God with cries of enthusiasm. We pleaded with God to be with us constantly in this new country. We prayed for his assistance and guidance so that we might make progress in our new surroundings faster than many refugees of our predecessors had. God heard our prayers and very soon our lives changed for the better. We learned to keep close to God through prayer, having discovered its power.

"Ask and it will be given to you; seek and you will find; knock and the door will be opened to you"

- MATTHEW 7:7, NIV

When you pray to God, He brings you a better answer without judging you based on your goodness, your height, your wealth or poverty.

I believe that God gives three succinct and immediate answers to our prayers of solicitation. Those answers are: yes; not right now; and I have something different and better than that you request.

If you go through a difficult period now, know that God is getting ready to bless you in a way that you can't imagine. God's instructions to me were to choose four people whom I wanted God to bless, and so I identified them.

When I think back upon how God has helped my family, I am reminded of other situations where God came to the aid of the hopeless. When Moses called upon God to part the Red Sea to allow the fleeing Israelites to escape their slave masters in Egypt, He answered. Jesus' revival of Lazarus, who had been dead for three days, is another example. Remember, though, that it is prayers to God for assistance in serving Him that are best.

"When you ask, you do not receive, because you ask with wrong motives, that you may spend what you get on your pleasures"

- JAMES 4:3, NIV

The following prayer is powerful. I ask you to pray it for all of us:

God, I ask you to bless my friends, parents, brothers and sisters, my co-workers and all those who read this now. Show them a new revelation about how to thank you for your plan for them and your promise. Amen.

Sisters and brothers, mothers, fathers, do not cease to hope.

Even when you fall on hard times or you feel like everything in the world is working against you. During good times, you may have turned your back on your heavenly father. Sometimes the Lord seems deaf to your voice, but sooner or later He will hear you and answer your prayers, so do not cease to hope.

You may constantly hear voices discouraging you, and you may want to give up hope, but the Bible says that there are three things that are eternal. Among these is faith in Christ. So keep the faith that one day you will be reunited with your heavenly father.

One day God will answer your prayers. So always have faith in the Lord.

WORD FROM JEAN CLAUDE MUSORE

"Your Promises Stand Forever" is my story of God's commitment to me, even through the hard times. When I was desperate for help, it was only He who delivered salvation.

I authored and published this book because God answered my prayers and has given me many blessings. In return, I promised to declare His goodness everywhere in the world. Nothing will prevent me from spreading His message. I do this because of my love for God and my faith in his plan for me. I have surrendered my life to His guidance and I will never quit.

"I will instruct you and teach you in the way you should go; I will counsel you with my loving eye on you"

-PSALM 32: 8, NIV

ABOUT AUTHOR

Jean Claude Musore was born in the Democratic Republic of Congo (DRC), formerly the Republic of Zaire, in a village called Vyura. He is the oldest of three children, and has two sisters.

On the 24th of December, 1997, Jean Claude accepted Jesus as his personal savior and was baptized at Bethel church in Uvira. In 2007, he came to California, where he currently lives.

He founded Ministries International, to proclaim the Kingdom of God to all mankind in order to help the many local Swahili speaking families who long for the familiar and important comfort of worship and social services in their native tongue.

Also he founder HMSV, Humura Mulenge Survivors and Victims to assisting his people in their efforts to rebuild their lives in the U.S. after suffering in their home countries.

He is now a writer and human rights advocate, living in California's Bay Area since his arrival in 2007. Jean Claude has authored short stories, essays, and monthly posts for Change.org's__human rights campaign.

For further information, contact:

Jmusore@hmsv.org

Phone: 510-533-3430

7549577R0

Made in the USA
Charleston, SC
16 March 2011